Katie Clemons
LET'S CELEBRATE YOUR STORY

BETWEEN
MOM
AND ME

A MOTHER ❤ SON
KEEPSAKE JOURNAL

 sourcebooks
jabberwocky

TO MY SPACEMAN MARTIN AND
ROCKET BOYS. NIKLAS AND LINDEN.
I LOVE YOU TO MIMAS AND BACK.

NIKLAS'S ART.
AGE 4

Published by Sourcebooks Jabberwocky, an imprint of Sourcebooks, Inc.
P.O. Box 4410, Naperville, Illinois 60567–4410
(630) 961-3900
Fax: (630) 961–2168
sourcebooks.com

Originally published in 2016 in the United States of America by Katie Clemons LLC.

Source of Production: Versa Press, East Peoria, Illinois, USA
Date of Production: June 2021
Run Number: 5022702

Printed and bound in the United States of America.
VP 14 13 12 11

A MOM'S PERSPECTIVE

It doesn't matter how long or difficult the day, any mother who glances at her sleeping son probably feels a tug of heartstrings. Trust me. It's nearly impossible to resist the bedside of my son, Niklas. I pull the blanket to his chin, close the book he fell asleep reading, or adjust the curtain so moonlight won't wake him. I look at the starry sky and know the old adage is true: I LOVE YOU TO THE MOON AND BACK.

There's something incredible about being a mom to a boy. I feel this deep desire to understand him. What makes him jump out of bed in the morning? Why would he pull up the covers and hide?

Kids get a notorious reputation for vaguely answering our attempts at conversation.

"How was your day?" we ask.

"Fine."

"Did you have a good time?"

"Yep."

Sometimes I'm eager to hear more from Niklas, and he's ready to share. We have the greatest conversations! But other days, the timing just isn't there. Either I'm primed to listen when he's not in the mood. Or worse, he wants to talk, while I confess I'm completely distracted: watching the road, thinking of what's for dinner, rushing to the next activity, and so forth. I'm not a very good listener in those moments—and he could be telling me something significant!

With the busy lives our families lead, I know it's often tricky to find the right circumstance for open dialogue or to know how to nurture your son's changing needs. Boys can also feel uncomfortable or embarrassed to share intimate things aloud—like "Hey Mom, I have armpit hair now!"

Yet sometimes a boy just needs you, his mom.

You are his definition of home, the place where he feels most confident and comfortable. As he learns to deal with life's challenges, he knows he has you behind him. When you deal with accidents and losses calmly, and treat others with kindness, you offer an example he can aspire to. His values, character, and sense of self-esteem are all things he learns from you. As he grows and opportunities come, he'll possess confidence to reach for the stars because you emboldened him.

Your son has craved opportunities to connect with you since you first held him in your arms. Sharing can be challenging, but this journal offers an inventive, lively way for you and your son to draw closer as you exchange stories, adventures, interests, and unique perspectives. As you answer prompts that make you laugh, reflect on each other's lives, or invite conversations on deeper issues, you and your son will launch into a more meaningful relationship.

Journaling is a lot like grasping a star chart while you gaze at the night sky. Without a chart, the sky feels vast, beautiful, and let's be honest—overwhelming. But when you hold a key, stars start coming together to form constellations and tell stories. The sky stops feeling so distant. In fact, you begin to feel more connected because you can identify patterns like Orion and Big Dipper.

I'll never forget the night when Niklas woke me when he was around four years old. As we stumbled to the bathroom, I reached for a light switch.

"No, Mommy," he whispered. "The moon is our night-light."

Let this journal be your star chart, your night-light as you navigate toward a closer relationship with your son. These five guideposts will help you get the most from your story-catching time together.

❶ WRITE YOUR OWN RULES.

Begin on the first page and work your way through this journal, or flip to any prompt that intrigues you and your son. Answer the questions together over mugs of hot chocolate or pass the book back and forth, making entries in turn. Write as much or as little as you want. Add or alter anything. Tear pages out or tape more in. If a prompt doesn't resonate with you, cross it out and write in your own, or cover it with a photograph, sticker, or drawing.

Your son's thoughts go on pages that begin "Dear Son" or "Son Writes." Corresponding "Dear Mom" and "Mom Writes" pages are your opportunity to reply or ignite another conversation. Intermixed throughout are spaces to doodle, write, and adhere keepsakes together.

❷ BECOME AN ENGAGED LISTENER.

Sharing this journal gives you and your son a glimpse inside one another's heads and hearts. Try to understand what your son is really communicating or how he's feeling. Does he need you to help him change something in his life, or is he just craving the chance to communicate while he sorts things out?

Some entries in this journal will address things you already know, while others can help you unearth emotions or entire stories you weren't aware of. Respond immediately or walk away and ruminate for a while. Also appreciate that your son may have stories he's not comfortable communicating yet. Be patient and keep listening.

❸ CONVEY YOUR HONEST iDEAS.

A story doesn't have to be perfect to be meaningful, and neither do you. Fill this journal with as many "I LOVE YOUS" or inside jokes as you want. Write what you know; admit what you don't. Model your values, and demonstrate to your son that imperfection and a sense of humor in both life and writing are okay.

I misspell words in my journal every time. There's an abundance of exclamation marks and crumbs from I don't know what. Once I discovered dozens of wobbly letter *N*s scrawled across the page (which Niklas still denies). But I keep going. If you try to edit as you go or plot a moral before beginning to journal, you unwittingly take away most of the raw truth and best discoveries that come from letting your pen wander across the page.

You just have to start.

❹ PLAY.

Think of this journal as your time capsule. It's a place for words; it's also a place to have fun! Doodle stick figures. Add speech bubbles and fake mustaches to illustrations. Write, underline, and circle words with different pens. Compose one entry sideways, then flip the page and write your next entry the other way. Snap pictures together and collect keepsakes, then adhere them with glue or double-sided tape. Above all, enjoy yourselves.

❺ GO BEYOND THESE PAGES.

Your mother-son journaling experience only begins with this journal. Come explore my exclusive *Between Mom and Me* resources, which include unexpected ways to swap top-secret messages in this book, journaling jokes your son will love, and examples from my own journals on:

KATIECLEMONS.COM/A/JBST

I'd love to hear how your journal is coming together. Please drop me a note at **howdy@katieclemons.com** (I answer all my mail) or join me on social media **@katierclemons**, **#katieclemonsjournals**, and **#betweenmomandme**.

Imagine picking up this journal in ten or twenty years or handing it to your grown son. You'll be taken back in time as you see pages filled with stories and perspectives that have long-since changed, youthful penmanship recording moments you haven't thought about in years, photographs, illustrations, and best of all...reminders of how much you love each other.

YOU'RE A GREAT MOM. Grab a blanket, spread it beneath the stars, and... Let's celebrate your story! ♡ Katie

Here's a photograph or drawing of

YOU  ME

HELLO **UNIVERSE!**

Our full names are

_____

_____

We call each other

_____

_____

We sign our names like this

_____

_____

We are _____ and _____ years old.

TODAY, WE LAUNCH THIS JOURNAL!

 Date_____

OUR JOURNAL
GUIDELINES

1 Is our journal top secret or can anyone else look inside?

2 If someone finds this journal, they should

☐ Return it

☐ Complete it

☐ Destroy it

☐ Share pages online

☐ Hide it in _____

☐ Sell it for $ _____

☐ Donate it to the local archives

3 Do we have to answer prompts in numerical order?

☐ Yes   ☐ No

❹ Our top focus(es) in this journal will be to

☐ Express our thoughts

☐ Use perfect grammar

☐ Capture memories

☐ Skip our responsibilities such as _____

_____ in order to write

☐ _____

☐ _____

❺ How much time do we have to write before passing our journal back to one another?

❻ What could we do if we need more space to write?

7 Is there a specific date when this journal must be complete?

8 How do we pass our journal back and forth?

9 How should we tell each other which page to turn to?

10 How can we communicate when we need an urgent response?

11 Are there other guidelines we should establish for our journal?

DEAR **MOM,**

What's something I do that makes you laugh?

MOM WRITES

DEAR **SON,**

What's something I do that makes you laugh?

TIME FOR A LAUGH!

YOU & ME

Our excited faces

MOM

SON

Our cranky faces

MOM

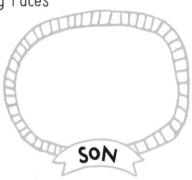
SON

Our goofy faces

MOM

SON

Date

DEAR
SON,

What are three of your most amazing accomplishments?

1

2

3

Is there another goal you want to achieve?

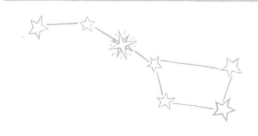

DEAR
MOM,

What are your thoughts on what I wrote
about my achievements?

What do you think of the goal I hope to accomplish?

SoN ☆ WRiTES

Mom, the first thing you say to me in the morning is

The last thing you say to me before bed is

MoM WRiTES

Son, the first thing you say to me in the morning is

The last thing you say to me before bed is

SON WRITES

Our family

Our community

Outside our house

Inside our house

MOM WRITES

Our family

Our community

Outside our house

Inside our house

Date

COOL THINGS WE'VE DONE

TOGETHER

1 _____

_____

_____

_____

2 _____

_____

_____

_____

3 _____

_____

_____

_____

4 _____

_____

_____

_____

AMAZING THINGS WE STILL NEED TO DO
TOGETHER

1

2

3

4

SoN ⭐ WRITES

Mom, you are beautiful inside and out because

1

2

3

4

5

SON WRITES

Here's a picture of you being

AWESOME, MOM.

MOM WRITES

Son, you are handsome inside and out because

1

2

3

4

5

Here's a picture of you being

AWESOME, SON.

SoN ⭐ WRiTES

I look forward to the holiday season because

_____

_____

_____

One of my favorite traditions is

_____

_____

_____

I remember one time when

_____

_____

_____

_____

_____

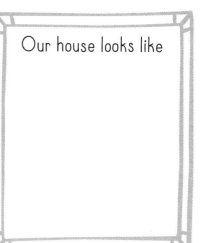

Our house looks like

Our house smells like

People who make the season magical

I love these food traditions

MOM WRITES

When I was growing up, I remember looking forward to the holiday season because

_____

_____

_____

One of my favorite traditions is

_____

_____

_____

I remember one time when

_____

_____

_____

_____

_____

_____

Our house looked like

Our house smelled like

People who made the season magical

I still cherish the memory of these foods

DEAR SON,

Tell me about a time you did something kind for someone else when you didn't have to.

AWESOME SPOT TO DRAW.

HIGH FIVE!

Why did you do it?

How did it make you feel?

35

DEAR MOM,

What are your thoughts on kindness?

GREAT SPOT
TO DOODLE.

Do you have a story of when you saw me being nice?

YOU & ME

Right now we're reading

MOM

SON

We're listening to

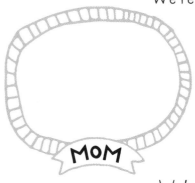

MOM

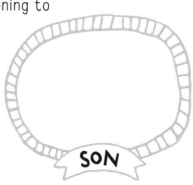

SON

We're watching

MOM

SON

WE WRITE

MOM WRITES

Son, I admire these traits in you

1 _____

_____

2 _____

_____

3 _____

_____

SON ✦ WRITES

Mom, I admire these traits in you

1 _____

_____

2 _____

_____

3 _____

_____

DEAR **MOM,**

What were you like when you were my age?
What was your life like?

DEAR **SON,**

How are you and your life different from
and similar to when I was a kid?

DEAR MOM,

Tell me a story or two about when I was little.

TIME TO SAY
"I LOVE YOU!"

DEAR
SON,

What do you think of girls?

How do you believe girls and women
deserve to be treated by men?

Do you ever see people doing something different?
How do you feel about that?

DEAR MOM,

What are your thoughts on what I wrote?

How do you believe girls and women
deserve to be treated by men?

Do you ever see people doing something different?
How do you feel about that?

Here's a picture of

YOU  & ME

relishing winter.

We give winter ☆☆☆☆☆ stars!

FILL IN FOR RATING.

- ☐ We love this season!
- ☐ Okay, winter gets kinda long.
- ☐ LET IT SNOW!
- ☐ We should move somewhere _____er.
- ☐ We have/haven't had enough snow days.
- ☐ Pour us another mug of _____.
- ☐ We can't feel our toes.
- ☐ Winter is warm here!
- ☐ _____

Brrrr!

Our winter theme song should be

The best things to do each winter are

1 _____

2 _____

3 _____

4 _____

5 _____

Date

DEAR MOM,

What are three of your most amazing accomplishments?

1

2

3

Is there another goal you want to achieve?

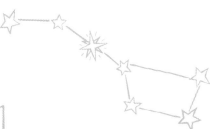

MOM WRITES

DEAR **SON,**

What do you think about the achievements I recorded?

TIME FOR APPLAUSE!

DEAR **MOM,**

Tell me about a special gift I made you when I was younger. Do you still have it?

Could you draw a picture?

DEAR
SON,

Date

What kinds of things do you like to make now?

Could you draw a picture?

YOU ♥ ME

Food we could eat forever

MOM

SON

Drinks we could guzzle all day

MOM

SON

Plug-your-nose gross food we hope we never eat again

MOM

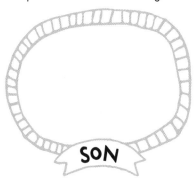

SON

WE WRITE

DEAR **SON,**

Date

What are four things you wish you could do?

1

2

3

4

DEAR MOM,

What do you think about the four things I wrote?

SUPER STAR
DOODLE AREA.

Was there anything you wished
you could do and then you did it ?

Mom, I know you love me so much because

Son, I know you love me so much because

DEAR **SON,**

Which school subject is difficult for you?

Why do you think it's so hard?

How can I help make it easier?

DRAW HOW YOU FEEL ABOUT IT.

DEAR **MOM,**

What are your thoughts on what I wrote about school?

PERFECT TIME FOR A HUG.

Which subject did you struggle with
when you were my age?

How does knowing that subject help your life today?

YOU & ME

Five things we can't live without

SON

MOM

DEAR MOM,

Would you tell me how I got my name?

DEAR SON,

I have a question for you

_____

_____

_____

GOOD TIME
TO SAY HOW
YOU FEEL!

★ ★ MOM WRITES ★ ★

Son, I always hear you say these phrases

★ ★ SON WRITES ★ ★

Mom, I always hear you say these phrases

MOM WRITES

Son, I'm proud of you because

_____
_____
_____
_____

I would describe you as a person who

_____
_____
_____
_____

You make me feel special when

_____
_____
_____
_____

SON WRITES

Mom, I'm proud of you because

_____

_____

_____

_____

I would describe you as a person who

_____

_____

_____

_____

You make me feel special when

_____

_____

_____

_____

DEAR MOM,

What are some of your favorite parts of being a parent?

NICE. SPOT
TO DOODLE. ANYWAY

DEAR
SON,

What do you think about what I wrote on being a parent?

Do you think you want to be a parent someday?

YOU ❤ ME

The happiest person we know

MOM

SON

The hardest-working person we know

MOM

SON

The funniest person we know

MOM

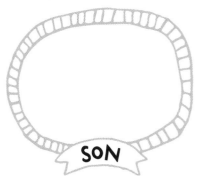

SON

DEAR **MOM,**

What was your first email address?

How did you get that name?

When did you get your first phone?

DRAW YOUR PHONE HERE.

Did your parents ever take away
your technology privileges? Why?

_____

_____

_____

_____

What did you do without today's technology?

_____

_____

DEAR **SON,**

Record your current email
or username here.

_____

How did you get that name?

_____

_____

_____

Which platforms do you use it for?

_____

_____

How do you use those platforms and how often?

_____

_____

_____

DRAW YOUR DEVICE HERE.

Do you ever feel pressured or
uncomfortable about anything online?

_____

_____

_____

_____

Is there anything I can do to help you when that happens?

_____

_____

DEAR **MOM,**

What are your thoughts on what I wrote
about feeling pressure or discomfort?

SON WRITES

Mom, in 30 years, you'll be ＿＿＿＿＿ years old. If you remember just one thing about who I am today, I hope it's

_____

_____

_____

_____

_____

MOM WRITES

Son, in 30 years, you'll be ＿＿＿＿＿ years old. If you remember just one thing about who I am today, I hope it's

_____

_____

_____

_____

_____

Here's a picture of
YOU & ME
doing something we love.

YOU ♥ ME

Date

Someone we'd love to meet

MOM

SON

Someone who's changed our lives

MOM

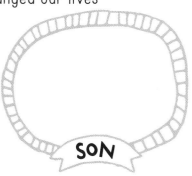

SON

Someone who's been a great friend this year

MOM

SON

WE WRITE   83

MOM WRITES

My typical weekday

6:00

7:00

8:00

9:00

10:00

11:00

NOON

1:00

2:00

3:00

4:00

5:00

6:00

7:00

8:00

9:00

10:00

SON WRITES

My typical weekday

6:00

7:00

8:00

9:00

10:00

11:00

NOON

1:00

2:00

3:00

4:00

5:00

6:00

7:00

8:00

9:00

10:00

DEAR MOM,

I have a question for you

_____

_____

_____

PERFECT TIME
FOR A HUG.

i ♥ u

Here's a picture of
YOU  ME
soaking up summer.

We give summer ☆☆☆☆☆ stars!

 FILL IN FOR RATING.

WE WRITE

- ☐ We love this season!
- ☐ Summer's just not long enough.
- ☐ LET THE SUN SHINE.
- ☐ The air conditioner is running.
- ☐ We should vacation somewhere _____ er.
- ☐ Give us all the icy _____ to drink.
- ☐ We own _____ bottles of sunblock.
- ☐ _____

Our summer theme song should be

The best things to do each summer are

1 _____

2 _____

3 _____

4 _____

5 _____

YOU ❤ ME

Our favorite shirts

MOM

SON

Our go-to shoes

MOM

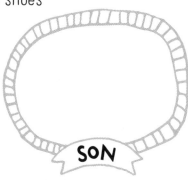

SON

Our goofiest piece of clothing

MOM

SON

DEAR **SON,**

Do you have any questions about growing up?

_____

_____

_____

_____

_____

_____

_____

Is there anything you feel nervous about?

_____

_____

_____

_____

_____

_____

DEAR **MOM,**

What do you think about what I just wrote?

MOM WRITES

ADD YOUR
DOODLES
HERE.

PERFECT TIME
FOR A HUG.

DEAR SON,

What sport do you enjoy?

What do you like about it?

How do you feel when you're doing it?

DEAR MOM,

What are your thoughts on sports
and what I just wrote?

MOM WRITES

Son, I'll always ask for your advice on

_____
_____
_____
_____

I've always appreciated how you

_____
_____
_____
_____

I hope that you never stop

_____
_____
_____
_____

SON WRITES

Mom, I'll always ask for your advice on

_____

_____

_____

_____

I've always appreciated how you

_____

_____

_____

_____

I hope that you never stop

_____

_____

_____

_____

YOU ♥ ME

What would we do if we had the whole day
together with no work or chores?

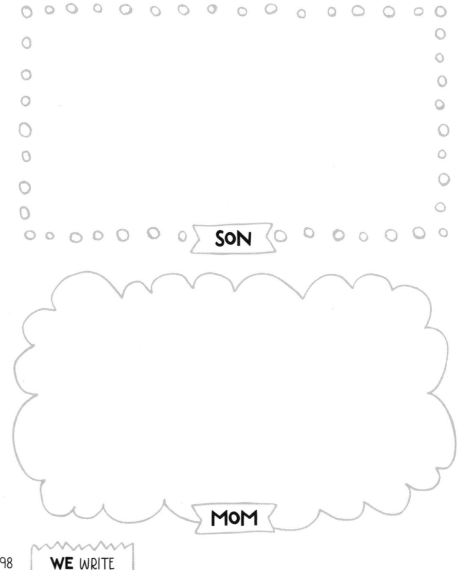

SON

MoM

YOU ♥ ME
WE'RE GRATEFUL FOR...

This place

This event on the calendar

This object in the house

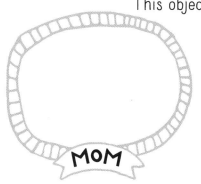

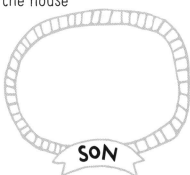

SON WRITES

My favorite **HOLIDAY** is

because _____

_____

_____

_____

_____

_____

Here's us **CELEBRATING!**

MOM WRITES

My favorite **HOLIDAY** is

because _____

_____

_____

_____

_____

_____

Here's us **CELEBRATING!**

DEAR **SON,**

Tell me about a hobby you enjoy.

How did you get interested in it?

What do you like about it?

What's challenging right now?

I give this hobby  stars!

FILL IN FOR RATING.

DEAR MOM,

Tell me about a hobby you enjoy.

How did you get interested in it?

What do you like about it?

What's challenging right now?

I give this hobby  stars!

FILL IN FOR
RATING.

SON  WRITES

Mom, this is you when

SOMEONE MAKES YOU LAUGH

YOU'RE IN YOUR ROOM

YOU DISCOVER I'VE WRITTEN
IN OUR JOURNAL

YOU GET A PACKAGE FROM

MOM WRITES

Son, this is you when

SOMEONE MAKES YOU LAUGH

YOU'RE IN YOUR ROOM

YOU DISCOVER I'VE WRITTEN
IN OUR JOURNAL

YOU GET A PACKAGE FROM

DEAR _____,

I have a question for you

_____

_____

_____

Date

SON WRITES

Here's a keepsake from my life right now

It's a

- ☐ ticket stub
- ☐ receipt
- ☐ wrapper
- ☐ newspaper clipping
- ☐ quote or poem
- ☐ list or note from my pocket
- ☐ photo or picture
- ☐ _____

I'm adding it to our journal because

MOM WRITES

Here's a keepsake from my life right now

It's a

☐ ticket stub

☐ receipt

☐ wrapper

☐ newspaper clipping

☐ quote or poem

☐ list or note from my pocket

☐ photo or picture

☐ _____

I'm adding it to our journal because

DEAR
SON,

Do you remember a story or two
from when you were little?

ADD YOUR
STORY
DOODLES HERE.

SON WRITES

The money we have has enabled our family to

_____

_____

_____

These are times when money doesn't matter to our family

_____

_____

_____

I think it's important to set aside money for

_____

_____

_____

I enjoy giving time or money to

_____

_____

_____

MOM WRITES

The money we have has enabled our family to

_____

_____

_____

These are times when money
doesn't matter to our family

_____

_____

_____

I think it's important to set aside money for

_____

_____

_____

I enjoy giving time or money to

_____

_____

_____

DEAR MOM,

What was your favorite job before I was born?

How old were you? And how much did you get paid?

How did you travel to work?

What were your responsibilities?

Why did you like the job?

Tell me about a mistake you made or lesson you learned.

DEAR **SON,**

What do you think about my favorite job?

Have you ever learned from a mistake that you made?

What kind of jobs do you want to experience?

Tell me about the kind of life you dream
of having when you're grown up.

DEAR **MOM,**

Tell me about an older relative that
I didn't get to know well.

ADD MEMORIES
AROUND THE
PICTURE FRAME.

SON WRITES

Two things you did that made me laugh
or smile this past week, Mom

1 _____

_____

2 _____

_____

Two things other people did that made me
happy this past week

1 _____

_____

2 _____

_____

Two things I did this past week that hopefully
brought other people joy

1 _____

_____

2 _____

_____

MOM WRITES

Two things you did that made me laugh
or smile this past week, Son

1

2

Two things other people did that made me
happy this past week

1

2

Two things I did this past week that hopefully
brought other people joy

1

2

YOU  ME

The view out our bedroom windows

MOM

SON

The things on our bedroom walls

MOM

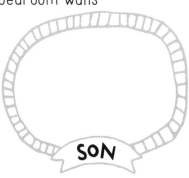

SON

The stuff on our bedroom floors

MOM

SON

DEAR **MOM,**

Tell me about the first time you held me.

SON WRITES
FUTURE PREDICTIONS

YOU AND ME IN _____ YEARS

Mom, I anticipate you won't have to spend
any more time on

_____

_____

_____

You'll have more time to

_____

_____

You'll be really good at

For your birthday, you'll want

I'll probably give you

I'll have to start reminding you to

Most likely, you'll still be reminding me to

We'll continue to tell each other

MOM WRITES
FUTURE PREDICTIONS

YOU AND ME IN _____ YEARS

Son, I anticipate you won't have to spend
any more time on

_____

_____

_____

You'll have more time to

_____

_____

You'll be really good at

For your birthday, you'll want

I'll probably give you

I'll have to start reminding you to

Most likely, you'll still be reminding me to

We'll continue to tell each other

★ SON WRITES ★

Mom, these foods always make me think of you.

★ MOM WRITES ★

Son, these foods always make me think of you.

YOU ♥ ME

Something we own that's red

MOM

SON

Something we've kept that's old

MOM

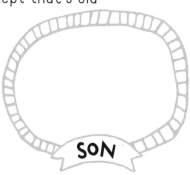

SON

Something we bought for ourselves

MOM

SON

MoM WRITES

Son, when you're _____ years old like I am now,

make sure you take time for yourself to

_____

_____

_____

_____

_____

_____

SoN WRITES

Mom, when I'm _____ years old like you are now,

make sure you take time for yourself to

_____

_____

_____

_____

_____

_____

DEAR MOM,

Do you vote?

What do you think makes a good candidate?

DEAR SON,

On a scale of 1 to 5, how do you feel about yourself?

How happy are you with your life?

Tell me more.

_____

_____

_____

_____

_____

_____

_____

_____

_____

_____

DEAR MOM,

What are your thoughts on what I just wrote?

DEAR _____,

I have a question for you

_____
_____
_____

WE WRITE

Son, let me trace your hand here.

SON WRITES

Mom, let me trace your hand here.

YOU ♥ ME

Give us an extra scoop of this ice cream

 **MOM**

 **SON**

When we've got the munchies, hand us a bowl of

 **MOM**

 **SON**

Cover our pizza with

 **MOM**

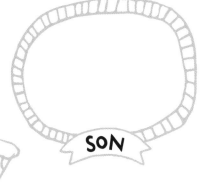 **SON**

DEAR
SON,

Tell me what else is on your mind.

Here's a picture of
YOU ♥ ME
being _____.

DEAR SON,

YAHOO! We've reached the end of this journal.
What did you enjoy about writing together?

How should we celebrate our journal's completion?

What will we do with our journal?

What do you want to do together next?

LET'S CELEBRATE YOUR STORY!

I believe that your story is one of the most
meaningful gifts you can give yourself and
the people you love. Thank you for entrusting
me and this journal with your adventures.
If you loved writing in these pages, let's celebrate
more of your story with my other books.
They're just as empowering and, well, awesome!

 LOVE, **MOM** AND **ME:** A Mother & Daughter Keepsake Journal

 BETWEEN **DAD** AND **ME:** A Father & Son Keepsake Journal

 LOVE, **DAD** AND **ME:** A Father & Daughter Keepsake Journal

 AWAITING **YOU:** A Pregnancy Journal

DISCOVER EVEN MORE KATIE CLEMONS
JOURNALS AT KATIECLEMONS.COM!